Sam and Pat
Beginning Reading and Writing

BOOK ONE

Jo Anne Hartel • Betsy Lowry • Whit Hendon

HEINLE
CENGAGE Learning™

Australia • Brazil • Japan • Korea • Mexico • Singapore • Spain • United Kingdom • United States

HEINLE
CENGAGE Learning™

Sam and Pat 1: Beginning Reading and Writing
Jo Anne Hartel, Betsy Lowry, Whit Hendon

Publisher, Adult and Academic: *James W. Brown*

Senior Acquisitions Editor, Adult and Academic:
Sherrise Roehr

Director of Product Development: *Anita Raducanu*

Editorial Assistant: *Katherine Reilly*

Director of Product Marketing: *Amy Mabley*

Senior Field Marketing Manager:
Donna Lee Kennedy

Product Marketing Manager: *Laura Needham*

Production Editor: *Erika W. Hokanson*

Print Buyer: *Mary Beth Hennebury*

Development Editor: *Julie Cormier*

Compositor: *Cadmus Communications*

Project Manager: *Andrea Clemente*

Illustrators: *Megan Purdum, Michael Roehr*

Cover Designer: *Lori Stuart*

Library of Congress Number: 2005930727

ISBN-13: 978-1-4130-1964-3

ISBN-10: 1-4130-1964-1

International Student Edition: 1-4130-1970-6

Heinle
25 Thomson Place
Boston, MA 02210
USA

Cengage Learning is a leading provider of customized learning solutions with office locations around the globe, including Singapore, the United Kingdom, Australia, Mexico, Brazil and Japan. Locate our local office at:
international.cengage.com/region

Cengage Learning products are represented in Canada by Nelson Education, Ltd.

Visit Heinle online at **elt.heinle.com**
Visit our corporate website at **cengage.com**

Contents

Acknowledgments

The inspiration for *Sam and Pat* came originally from Sylvia Greene, whose basal reader, *Sam and Val,* is the model for our work. In fact, we would never have conceived of *Sam and Pat* without Sylvia's encouragement and permission to use her ideas and her main character, Sam.

We would especially like to acknowledge Joann Wheeler, the talented artist who did the original drawings for this work. With deftness and simplicity, she breathed life into the characters and helped to make the stories more real for the readers.

This work would not have been possible without the funding and ongoing support of the Massachusetts Department of Education and everyone involved in the YALD Project. Special thanks go to Ashley Hager, Allyne Pecevich, Sheila Petruccelli, and Betty Stone, who helped us produce the first version of the book. Many thanks to Bob Bickerton and Jackie Fletcher as well as for their continual support throughout the project.

We would also like to thank those people who provided us with essential knowledge about the reading process. Like many other English language teachers working in adult basic education, we are always trying to come up with good materials and techniques for teaching English language learners at the beginning literacy levels. The YALD Theory and Practice in Reading Course, designed for teachers in the Boston area by John Strucker, gave us much needed background in teaching reading and exposure to a variety of teaching materials and methods. In addition, we would also like to thank Barbara Wilson for her Wilson Reading System, which informed our writing of the stories and our teaching.

Thanks to our colleagues at the Community Learning Center, who helped us all along the way and contributed ideas to this project. Special thanks to Ann Haffner for her suggestions, expertise, and ideas for organizing the book, and to John Galli, whose early contributions and enthusiasm kept us moving. Our gratitude goes to Mina Reddy, who helped us find time in our schedules to write the stories. Thanks also to proofreaders, Deb Foxx and Linda Huntington.

And last but certainly not least, we would also like to thank our students at the Community Learning Center, whose determination to learn to speak, read, and write English was the motivation for *Sam and Pat.* Their reactions to the stories and exercises as well as their contributions to the storyline were invaluable.

References

Kaufman, Lorna M., Ph.D., and Pamela E. Hooks, Ph.D. "The Dyslexia Puzzle, Putting the Pieces Together." New England Branch of the Orton Dyslexia Society, 1996.

Rosewell, Florence G. and Jeanne S. Chall. *Reading Difficulties, Effective Methods for Successful Teaching.* Elizabethtown, PA.: Continental Press, 1999.

Rosewell, Florence G. and Jeanne S. Chall. *Creating Successful Readers, A Practical Guide to Testing and Teaching at All Levels.* Itasca, IL.: The Riverside Publishing Company, 1994.

Schwarz, R. and L. Terrill. "ESL Instruction and Adults with Learning Disabilities." ERIC Digest. National Clearinghouse for ESL Literacy Education, Washington, DC. ED#EDO-LE-00-01 (June 2000).

Snow, C. and J. Strucker. "Lessons from preventing reading difficulties in young children for adult learning and literacy." *Annual Review for Adult Learning and Literacy* 1 (2000): 25-69.

Introduction

Sam and Pat is a basal reading series designed for English language learners who do not read or write in English. Some English language learners have little formal education and limited literacy skills in their native languages. Others come from countries that do not use the Roman alphabet, and still others have additional problems that could be the result of learning disabilities. All are struggling to learn English for the first time. Students at the most basic level are not yet comfortable holding a pencil and are slow or awkward when they are trying to write. *Sam and Pat* is intended to help beginning English language readers understand the alphabetic principle, that letter symbols represent sounds and that the sounds of the letters can be blended to make words. In addition, the stories in this book contain many words that the students are expected to learn as sight words. They are not to be learned by applying phonics but rather by remembering how they look.

Sam and Pat is a collection of stories, which follows a sequence of phonics skills. The actual phonics sequence appears in the lesson chart after this introduction. Each lesson starts with a picture or picture story that introduces the topic and new vocabulary. The stories are followed by comprehension and phonics exercises. The storyline of the book is loosely woven together since all the lessons are about family of the main characters, Sam and Pat.

Sam and Pat addresses some specific needs of English language learners:

1. The phonics sequence has been adjusted for English language learners who often have difficulty pronouncing and distinguishing certain sounds. For example, when an exercise requires the student to hear the difference between two sounds, the sounds first chosen are very different from each other. In a later lesson, one of the sounds is contrasted again with another that is more similar. The level of difficulty in exercises increases slowly.

2. Only simple words that students might encounter in their daily lives are used in the stories because literacy students have a limited vocabulary in English.

3. The stories are written with simplified grammar since long sentences and complex structures can interfere with comprehension.

4. Simplified themes from daily life have been incorporated into the stories because discussion of abstract ideas is not always possible when students' language skills are limited.

English Language Learners

English language learners sometimes have learning difficulties. These may be due to learning disabilities, a lack of exposure to English, unfamiliarity with the conventions of school, little or no facility with language learning, or a combination of these factors. Learning disabilities might be confused or obscured by issues connected with acquiring a new language. For example, a student might have trouble repeating back a sentence of more than three or four words because of phonological or auditory deficits. However, the problem may also be caused by limited educational background or lack of exposure to spoken English. English language learners bring different learning styles and abilities to the classroom. Some learn visually, while others need to interact with material by physically manipulating it. *Sam and*

Pat is meant for all beginning English readers and writers. The materials lend themselves to lessons that include listening, oral work, and hands-on activities, for example, with flash cards. Learners who have no learning disabilities will most likely be able to progress more quickly through the material than those who have learning disabilities.

The Lessons

Sam and Pat is designed for instruction in the following skills:

- Phonics
- Vocabulary
- Sight words
- Oral reading for accuracy
- Oral reading for fluency
- Silent reading
- Reading comprehension

Although the language in the stories is simple, some advance work is needed to clarify vocabulary and to introduce new concepts before the students actually read a lesson. *Sam and Pat* is only *one* component of an English language learner curriculum. Because the book focuses primarily on reading and writing, the material can be expanded with supplementary listening and speaking activities. The **Lesson Chart** lists the phonics skills and sight words covered in each lesson, as well as suggested vocabulary, grammar, and discussion topics.

Other Materials

In addition to the text, teachers may want to have other materials on hand, such as:

- The *Sam and Pat* audio program (available in CD or cassette format) for listening to the lesson stories
- A set of flash cards for key word pictures and letters for students to learn the sounds and names of the letters
- Sets of flash cards with sight words, one for each student to use
- Sets of letter cards for making words
- Cards with pictures on one side and corresponding words on the other for learning new words
- Separate picture and corresponding word cards for matching activities
- Sentences cut into words or phrases for students to put in order

Teaching Suggestions

Phonics for Reading

Phonics involves teaching the sounds of letters and then blending the sounds to make words. This skill is necessary for both reading and writing. Each lesson in *Sam and Pat* contains a target sound or sounds. Refer to the **Phonics** column in the Lesson Chart on pp. xii-xiii for the target sounds in each lesson.

Suggested Additional Materials

- **Key Word Cards for Phonics** See the pictures on pp. 110-112 for key words and sounds. These can be glued to 3 x 5 index cards and laminated. Every sound presented in the book should have a card (e.g., /e/, /th/, /ea/, /z/, etc.) Display the cards on the board tray or in a pocket chart. An ideal way to use these cards, if a magnetic board is available, is to attach magnetic tape to the backs of the cards so that they will stick to the board. For each card, say the name of the letter or letters, then the key word, and finally the sound. It is important to clip the pronunciation of the sounds; i.e., /p/ should remain voiceless and not pronounced "puh". /m/ is pronounced "mmm…" and not "muh." Review the names of the letters, key words, and their corresponding sounds for a few minutes in each class session.

- **Letter Cards** Make available to students sets of cards with individual letters. Make cards for consonants—b, c, d, f, g, h, j, k, l, m, n, n, p, qu, r, s, t, v, w, x, y, z, th, ch, sh, ck. Put vowels—a, e, i, o, u, ee, ea, ai, ay—on cards of a different color.

Suggested Activities

Select 10-12 phonetically regular words from your current lesson and previous lessons. Practice these words in a variety of ways.

- Write the words on flash cards or on the board. For each word, point to each letter and say the individual sounds. Then run your finger under the word as you say it to show students how to blend the sounds. Students repeat, then practice chorally and individually.

- Students can study their word cards independently or use them to quiz each other.

- Write the words on the board. Point to a word and ask for the letter that makes a certain sound. For example, in the word *mat*: What letter says /t/? What letter says /a/?

- Write the list of words on the board. Students read chorally and independently. Erase the first letter of a word, say the word, and students say the name of the letter that is missing. Proceed through the list, erasing initial consonants. Continue by erasing the last letters, and students again provide the names of the missing letters.

- Use letter cards for reading. Lay out letter cards to make words. Students read the words as a group and individually as you lay them out.

- Select a series of words that differ by one sound; e.g., *cat, cap, tap, top, mop,* etc. With the letters on the board tray, table, or magnetic board, ask students to read the words as you take out a letter and substitute a new one, progressing through the list.

Phonics for Spelling

Suggested Activities

- Use the **Key Word Cards for Phonics** on pp. 110–112 to reinforce the spelling of words in each lesson. Say the sound, and students respond with the name of the letter or letters that correspond to the sound.

- Have students use letter cards to form words. Dictate words with the target sound or sounds. If magnetic letters are available, students come to the board, and put words together as you dictate them. If individual sets of letter cards are used, students can do the same activity independently or in pairs.

- Select a series of words that differ by one sound (*cat, cap, tap, top, mop*). Students make words with the letter cards, substituting letters as you dictate new words.

Writing Exercises in *Sam and Pat*

Phonetic Word Grids

These grids, found on pp. 103–109, give students extra practice in identifying and writing phonetic words. Each grid corresponds to a lesson. Refer to the *Phonics* column in the **Lesson Chart** on pp. xii-xiii for the sequence of sounds. Review the pictures in the grid with students to make sure they understand the vocabulary and can interpret the pictures correctly. Read the list of words at the top of the page with students before assigning a grid.

"Listen and write the missing letters" activities

These activities are noted in the book by this icon: 🗩. You can use the **Suggested Listening Scripts** on pp. 113–114, or you can choose your own words. Choose phonetically regular words from the current lesson or previous lessons to dictate to students. The class repeats each word before filling in the missing sound. The sounds of the missing letters should be limited to ones that have already been taught.

"Listen and write" activities

These activities are also noted in the book by this icon: 🗩. You can use the **Suggested Listening Scripts** on pp. 113–114, or you can choose your own words. Again choose words from the lesson that contain the target sound. They can be the same words as in the "*Listen and write the missing letters*" activities. Students repeat the words before they write them. Students then read back the words that they have written.

"Circle the word you hear" activities

These activities are also noted in the book by this icon: 🗩. You can use the **Suggested Listening Scripts** on pp. 113–114, or you can choose your own words. Decide in advance which words students will circle, one word in each line. The class repeats the word you say before they circle it. At the end of the exercise, students read back the words that they circled.

Read/Write

Students read the list of words; e.g., in "Sam is Late to Work," *run, fun, gum, sun,* etc. Focus attention on the target sound /u/ by asking what letter is the same in all the words. Students repeat and then read the words as a group and individually. Ask for the number of the word you say. "What number is *sun*?" "What number is *hug*?" Ask students to read the list again in pairs or as a group.

Vocabulary and Sight Words

Some of the words in each lesson need to be recognized on sight. Some are new vocabulary words, and some are high frequency reading words. In both cases, they are not taught in the same manner as phonetically regular words because they are not phonetically regular (e.g., *the, are,* or *do*), or they have sounds not yet introduced. Sight words and vocabulary appear in the *New Sight Words* and *Suggested Vocabulary and Grammar Topics* sections in the **Lesson Chart** on pp. xii-xiii. Introduce these new words a few at a time and review old ones in every class session before reading a story.

Suggested Activities for Vocabulary

- Use pictures from the book, line drawings, photographs, and real objects. Students point to a picture, drawing, photograph, or real object as you say a word. Limit the number of words covered in each class session to no more than eight.
- Make flash cards with pictures and corresponding flash cards with words for students to match. As this set of cards grows, review.
- Play games with the flash cards. Give a definition or description of the word and have students pick out the correct flash card.
- Students sort cards according to topic; for example, days of the week, numbers, or family members.
- Play bingo with pictures and words.
- Give students a cloze exercise to fill in new vocabulary.
- Give students a worksheet with pictures to label.

Suggested Activities for Sight Words

- Present five to eight new sight words at a time.
- Review sight words from previous lessons.
- Write a sight word on the board in large letters. Say the word for students. Students repeat it. With an arm and index finger extended straight, demonstrate how to write the word in the air, while looking at the board and spelling the word out loud. Students do the same. Erase the word from the board, and students write it again in the air, spelling it aloud. Students pretend to write the word a third time with their finger on the table. Finally, they write it in their notebooks.
- Students keep a section in their notebooks for sight words.
- Using flash cards or the sight words written in their notebooks, students read, cover, spell aloud, and then write each word.
- Choose a combination of old and new sight words to dictate to students.

Reading and Reading Comprehension

Pre-reading

- Before reading a story, practice related grammar and content orally. Use the *Suggested Vocabulary and Grammar Topics* and the *Suggested Discussion Topics* from the **Lesson Chart** to plan listening and speaking activities that relate to the lesson. For example, before reading Lesson 9, "Sam Can't Get Up," review telling time, and teach daily routines and the present tense. Use dialogs, role-plays, and pictures for listening and speaking practice.

- Each lesson begins with an illustration or picture story. Discuss the picture or series of pictures with students, eliciting the story line and checking for comprehension of new words and topics. Students might label the pictures, copying words from the board. Help students to understand the story by relating it to their own experiences. After talking about an individual introductory illustration, ask the class to predict what will happen in the story.

Reading for Accuracy and Fluency

Students need many opportunities to practice so that they can read accurately and smoothly.

- Read the story aloud to the class and then have students read aloud. Individuals can take turns reading parts of the story.

- While students are reading the text, have them follow along by tracing under the words with the eraser end of a pencil or a finger.

- Encourage students to speed up and read more naturally by reading chunks of text consisting of two or three words at a time.

- Have pairs of students work together, reading to each other.

Reading Comprehension

A variety of activities and exercises help students develop comprehension skills.

- Cut up sequenced story illustrations. Give a set to individuals or pairs, who then put the pictures in the order of the story.

- Give students sentences from the story on strips of paper. They match pictures from the story to the sentence strips.

- Students put the sentence strips in the order of the story.

- Cut sentence strips in half and pass them out to individuals. Students match the sentence pieces by walking around the classroom and finding their partners.

- The class acts out dialogs or scenes from a story in pairs or small groups. Props, such as hats can help students get into character. Old telephones are useful in acting out situations such as phoning to make a doctor's appointment.

Sample Lesson

Book 1, Lesson 19: Sam Gets a Job

Objectives	Activities	Materials
1. **Conversation/Vocabulary/Critical Thinking** Students discuss their skills and abilities at home and at work.	Make a chart with a column for students' names and another for actions: i.e., *sew, drive, speak English, cook, sing,* etc. Brainstorm abilities and match to individual students. Students make sentences about themselves using *can*. If there is time, students write some sentences about themselves.	Flash cards with pictures of actions and corresponding word cards
2. Students tell the story in Lesson 19 and learn new vocabulary: *bag, stock*	Students identify actions in the story, repeat sentences, and tell the story by looking at the pictures.	Introductory picture story in Lesson 19
3. **Phonics** Review the sounds /qu/, /r/, /j/, /g/, /w/, /ch/, /sh/, /ck/, /c/, /k/, short vowels	Use Key Word Cards for Phonics. Class works as a group. Students give the names of the letters, the key word, and then the sound of the letters.	Key Word Cards for Phonics
4. Review of words with short vowels and **st** blend: *can, boss, shop, mop, job, bag, well, think, hot, hat, hit, him, hum, hem, sock, stock, stick, sick*	Make words with letter cards. Students read the words by blending the sounds of the letters.	Flash cards with letters that can be strung together to form words
5. **Sight words** Students learn new sight words: *market, start, Monday, then, forgot, pay, maybe, talks*	Students "sky write," trace, copy words into their binders and on to their own packs of file cards for sight words.	Flash cards with sight words; file cards
6. **Oral Reading** Practice reading aloud, decoding.	The class reads the story aloud as a group and practices for fluency in pairs.	Copies of Lesson 19
7. **Reading Comprehension and Making Inferences**	Work on comprehension of the story orally. Ask: How does Sam feel? Do you think this is a good job for Sam? Why did he forget to ask how much the pay is?	Copies of comprehension questions for Lesson 19
8. **Writing/Phonics** Students review the spelling of the sounds: /qu/, /r/, /j/, /w/, /g/, /ch/, /sh/, /ck/, /c/, /k/, /b/, short vowels	"What says…?" Give the sound of a letter, and the students give the name of the letter.	Key Word Cards for Phonics
9. Students spell words with short vowel sounds and **st** blend.	Dictate a word, and students make words with letter cards: *stop, shop, mop, cop, Pat, pit, pot, not, nut, net, sick, stick*	Sets of letter cards for individuals or pairs of students to use
10. Students practice writing words with short **o** and **st**.	Students fill out worksheets.	Spelling exercises for Lesson 19

Lesson Chart

Lesson	Phonics	New Sight Words	Vocabulary and Grammar Topics	Suggested Discussion Topics
1 Sam and Pat	• Consonants: initial/final sounds; **s, m, p, t, f, g, c, d, h, n** • Vowels: short **a** (Phonetic Word Grid 1)	they, this, not, married, home, are, good, cook, happy, is, and, at	• Verb **to be** (present) • Subject pronouns (I, she, he)	• Introductions • Adjectives • Describing pictures
2 The Van	• Consonants: initial/final sounds; **b, v, r, k, w** • Vowels: short **a**	his, her, work, please, go, in, to, the, a, if, class, asks, you	• Possessive adjectives • His/her • **Have to** • **Can/can't** (permission & ability)	• "I have to…" • "Can I?" • Transportation • Men and women
3 At Home	• Consonants: **l, j, qu, x, y, z** • Vowels: short **a**	she, today, day, off, Tuesday, salad, too	• He/she • Days of the week • **When (with you, she, he)**	• Daily/weekly routines • Work schedules • Food and cooking
4 Sam Is Late to Work	• Vowels: short **u** (Phonetic Word Grid 2)	late, boss, very, on, he, fast	• Time • Numbers	• Work culture • Problems on the job • Transportation
5 Sam Has a Problem	• Consonants: review • Vowel contrast: short **a**, short **u** (Phonetic Word Grid 3)	problem, early, what, do	• Time • Numbers	Time
6 Gus	• Consonants: review • Vowel contrast: short **a**, short **u**	friend, taxi, thank you, says, with	• 3rd person present "s" **(says, has)**	Friends
7 Football **8** The Ball Is In!	• **ll, ss, ff** • **all** • **ck**	football, game, last, Sunday	• Adjectives describing people • Review **can/can't** (ability)	Sports
9 Sam Can't Get Up	• Consonants: review initial sounds	house, come, get up, here	• Contractions **(can't, it's)** • Get up • Hurry up	• Daily routines • Getting up
10 Sam Is up Fast	Consonants: digraphs - **sh**	wash, put, pants, shirt, socks, shoes, jacket	• **Have to** • Clothing • **Put on**	Morning routines
11 Pat Shops on Saturday	Final **s**	Saturday, chicken, milk, lunch, sale, put	• Plurals • Review 3rd person present tense	Market

Lesson	Phonics	New Sight Words	Vocabulary and Grammar Topics	Suggested Discussion Topics
12 Pat's Job	• Consonants: digraphs - **ck** • Vowels: short **i** (Phonetic Word Grid 4)	school, lunch, for, stink, job, sticks, ick	• Jobs • Future with **will**	• Jobs • Meals
13 Go Home, Sam	• Consonants: final sounds • Digraphs - **ch** • Vowels: review short **a, u, i**	fired, matter, kitchen, Friday, no, I'm	• Contractions: **to be** (I'm you're...)	• Job problems • Workers' rights and responsibilities
14 It Is Very Expensive	• Vowels: short **e** • Review short **a** (Phonetic Word Grid 5)	bill, expensive, need, heat, telephone, December, who, rent	• "Get off my back" • Months • **Who** questions • **Is/are** (The rent **is**..., The bills **are**....)	• Money problems • Paying bills • Living expenses
15 Gus and Sam Relax **16** Fish Smell	• Review - **sh, ch, th, ck**	relax, small, smell, your, take	• Present tense • Possessive adjectives (**their, your,** etc.)	• Spare time
17 Buddy	• Vowels: short **e** • Vowel contrast: short **e** and short **u**	son, name, trumpet, lesson, every, Wednesday, night, play	Family	• Family • Raising children • Hobbies
18 What Can Sam Do?	• Vowels: review short **a, i, u**	things, different, clean, people, hands	**Can, can't**	• Getting a job • Skills
19 Sam Gets a Job	• Consonants: blends - **st** • Vowels: short **o** (Phonetic Word Grid 6)	market, start, Monday, then, forgot, pay, maybe, talks	• **What** questions • Jobs • Interviews	• Wages • Job duties • Applications • Job ads • Interviews
20 Sam Tells Pat the Good News	• Consonants: blends - **st, sl, sm, sp** (Phonetic Word Grid 7) • Vowels: review short **o** • Vowel contrast: short **o, a, u, i, e**	news, time, from, stay, oh	• Review **who** and **what** questions • Jobs • "Oh, no!" (expression)	• Job duties • Questions and answers • Dialogues
21 Pat Is in New York	• Vowel contrast: short **a, o**	New York, brother, see, thanks, love	• Asking for directions • Review **have to/has to**	Transportation
22 Sam Has a Pain in His Back	• Review: final **s** • **-ing**	have, don't	• Review future with **will**	Health

 Sam and Pat

🎧 1. This is Sam.

2. This is Pat.

3. They are Sam and Pat.

4. Sam and Pat are married.

5. They are at home.

6. Sam is fat.

7. Sam is a fat man.

8. Pat is not fat.

9. Pat is a good cook.

10. Pat and Sam are happy.

Circle the answer.

1. This is
   Sam.

   Pat.

2. This is
   Sam.

   Pat.

3. Sam is
   sat.

   fat.

4. Sam and Pat are
   happy.

   sad.

Listen and write the missing letters.

1. ____am

2. ____at

3. ____at

4. ____an

5. Sa____

6. Pa____

7. fa____

8. ma____

Listen and write.

1. _____

2. _____

3. _____

4. _____

5. _____

Lesson

(2) The Van

1. Pat has a van.

2. It is her van.

3. Pat can go to work in her van.

4. Pat is happy in her van.

5. Sam has to go to class.

6. Sam can't have the van.

7. It is not his van.

8. Sam asks, "Can I have the van?"

9. Sam asks, "Please, can I go to class in the van?"

10. "No, you can't."

11. "I have to go to work."

Write *Yes* or *No*.   **Yes or No**

1. Sam and Pat have a van.   _____

2. Pat has a class.   _____

3. Sam has work.   _____

4. The class is at 9:00.   _____

5. Work is at 9:00.   _____

6. Pat asks, "Can I have the van?"   _____

Circle the /a/ sound in each word.

1. van   5. class   9. man

2. happy   6. at   10. Sam

3. can't   7. asks   11. Pat

4. has   8. can   12. fat

Listen and write the missing letters.

1. ____an   6. can'____

2. ____an   7. ha____

3. ____an   8. va____

4. ____lass   9. goo____

5. ____as   10. coo____

Lesson

3 At Home

1. Sam and Pat are at home.

2. It is Tuesday.

3. Pat is happy.

4. It is her day off.

5. Today she can cook.

6. Pat is a good cook.

7. She can cook a ham and yams.

8. They can have a salad too.

Write *Yes* or *No*.   **Yes or No**

1. Pat and Sam are at work.   _____

2. It is Thursday.   _____

3. Pat has a day off.   _____

4. Sam can cook.   _____

5. Pat can cook a ham.   _____

Circle the words you hear.

1. hat   ham   has

2. rag   rat   rap

3. cat   cap   can

4. have   ham   hat

5. map   mat   man

6. Pat   Pam   pad

7. at   am   an

8. sad   sack   Sam

9. bag   bad   bat

10. tan   tack   tap

**Write the missing letter _a_ in each word.
Read the words.**

1. h____m

2. y____m

3. S____m

4. P____t

5. f____t

6. ____t

7. h____t

8. b____d

9. s____d

10. m____d

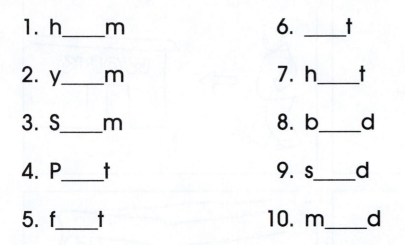

Write the words you hear.

1. _____

2. _____

3. _____

4. _____

5. _____

6. _____

Lesson

(4) Sam Is Late to Work

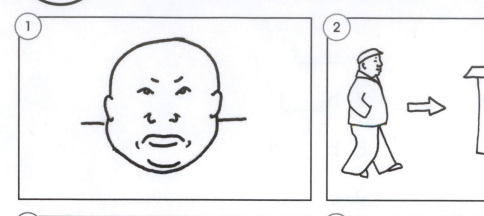

1. Sam is mad. He is very mad.

2. He has to go to work.

3. And he can't have the van.

4. Sam has to go to work on the bus.

5. The bus is not fun. The bus is not fast.

6. Sam has to go to work at 9:00 A.M.

7. The bus is not fast. It is 9:15 A.M.

8. Sam has to run. He is late.

9. Sam is late to work.

10. The boss is very mad at Sam.

Fill in the blanks with these words.

mad   fast   van   work   run

1. Sam has to go to _____.

2. Sam can't have the _____.

3. The bus is not _____.

4. Sam is late. He has to _____.

5. The boss is very _____.

Read.   **Write.**

1. run   1. _____

2. fun   2. _____

3. gum   3. _____

4. sun   4. _____

5. rug   5. _____

6. mug   6. _____

7. bug   7. _____

8. hug   8. _____

Lesson

5 Sam Has a Problem

1. Sam has a problem.

2. His work is at 9:00 A.M.

3. Pat has the van.

4. Sam has to go to work on the bus.

5. The 7:30 A.M. bus is early.

6. The 9:30 A.M. bus is late.

7. And the bus is not fast.

8. Sam is not happy.

9. The bus is not fun.

10. What can Sam do?

Write *Yes* or *No*.

1. Sam has work at 9:00 A.M.   _____

2. Sam has to go to work on the bus.   _____

3. The bus is fast.   _____

4. The bus is fun.   _____

5. Sam is happy.   _____

Pick the correct word. Fill in the blanks.

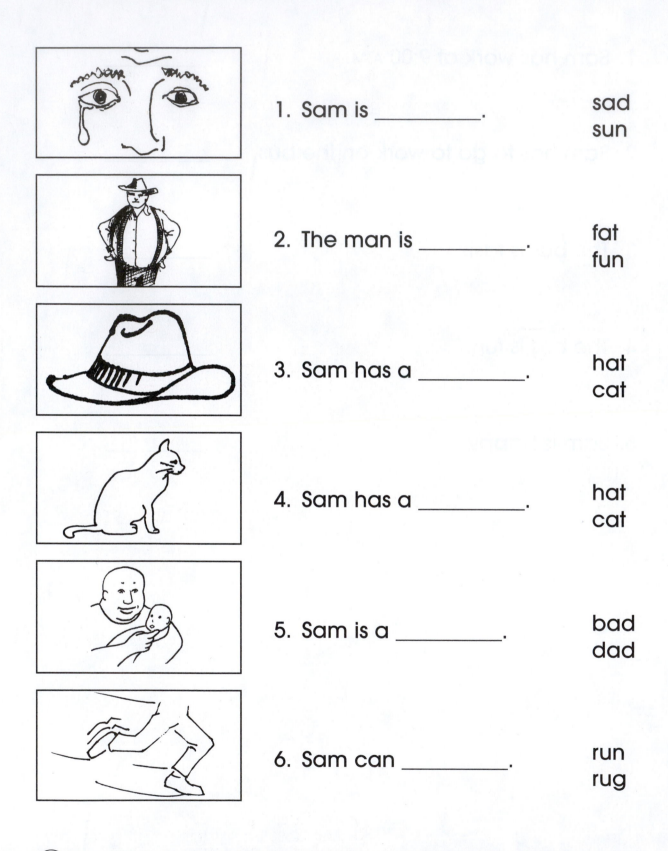

1. Sam is _____.

    sad
    sun

2. The man is _____.

    fat
    fun

3. Sam has a _____.

    hat
    cat

4. Sam has a _____.

    hat
    cat

5. Sam is a _____.

    bad
    dad

6. Sam can _____.

    run
    rug

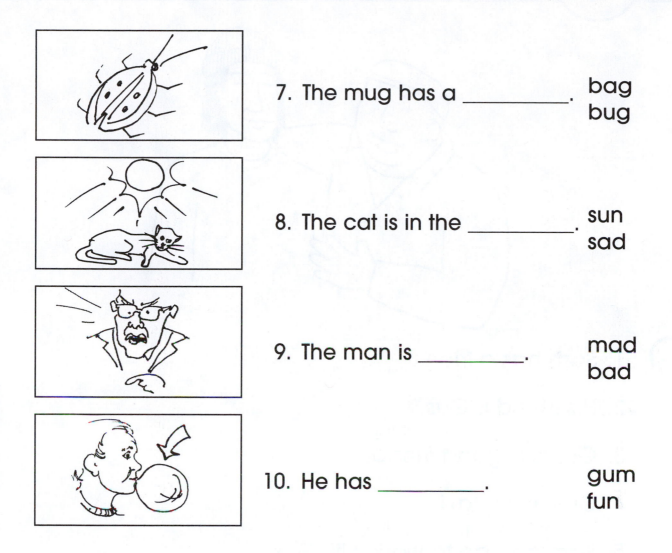

7. The mug has a _____.   bag
                                 bug

8. The cat is in the _____.   sun
                                     sad

9. The man is _____.   mad
                              bad

10. He has _____.   gum
                          fun

Lesson

6 Gus

1. Sam has a friend.

2. His friend is Gus.

3. Gus is a good friend.

4. Gus has a taxi.

5. Sam can go to work with Gus.

6. Sam can go with Gus in the taxi.

7. Gus can get Sam at 8:15.

8. Sam is very happy.

9. Sam says, "Thank you, Gus."

10. "Thank you. You are a very good friend."

Write *Yes* or *No*.   *Yes* or *No*

1. Sam has a friend.   _____

2. Gus has a bus.   _____

3. Gus has a taxi.   _____

4. Pat can go to work in the taxi.   _____

5. Gus can get Sam at 8:15.   _____

Write the words that have /a/.

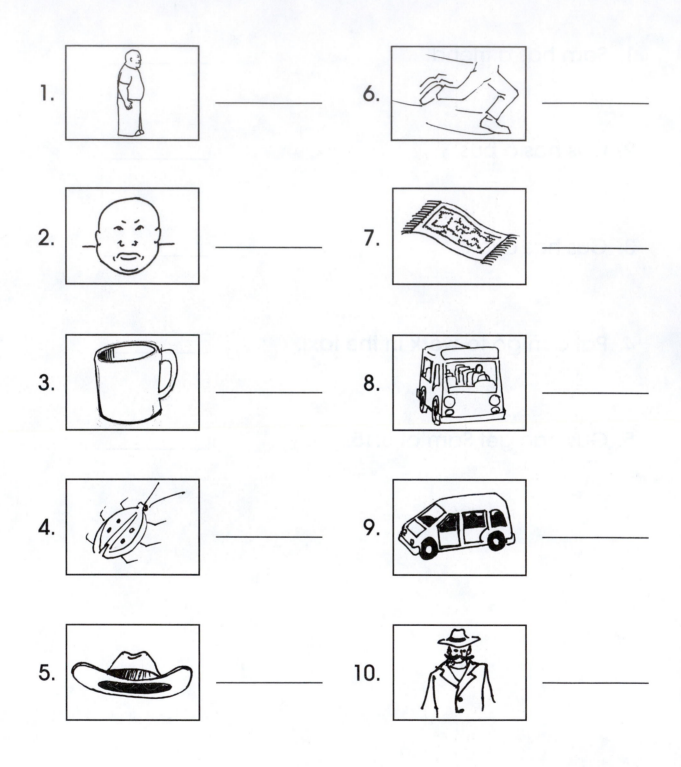

1. _____

2. _____

3. _____

4. _____

5. _____

6. _____

7. _____

8. _____

9. _____

10. _____

Write the words. The words all have /u/.

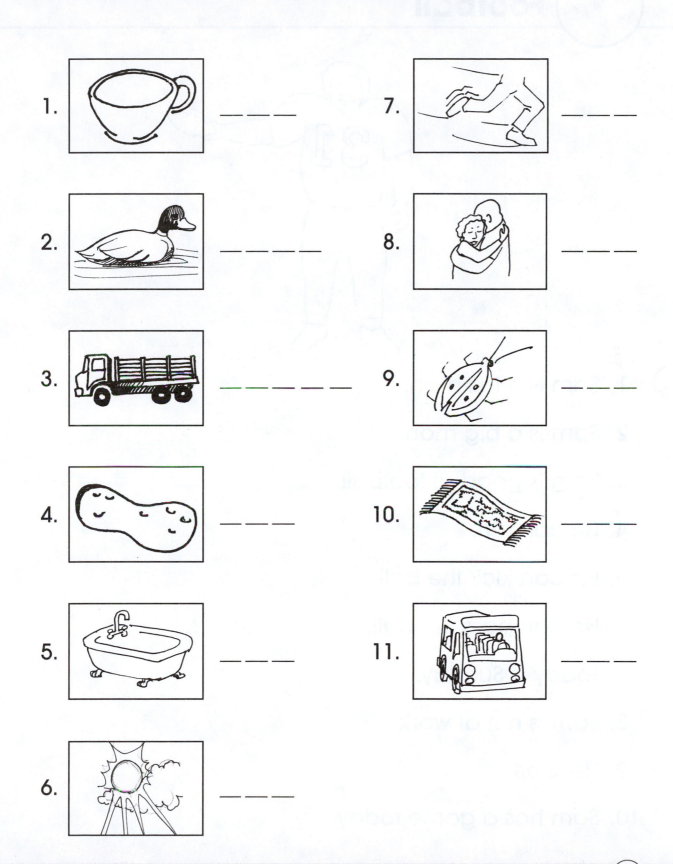

1. _ _ _

2. _ _ _

3. _ _ _ _ _

4. _ _ _

5. _ _ _

6. _ _ _

7. _ _ _

8. _ _ _

9. _ _ _

10. _ _ _

11. _ _ _

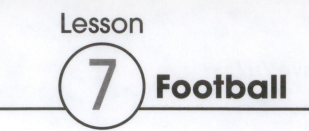

1. Sam is a tall man.

2. Sam is a big man.

3. Sam is good at football.

4. He can run.

5. He can kick the ball.

6. He can pass the ball.

7. Today is Sunday.

8. Sam is not at work.

9. He is off.

10. Sam has a game today.

Fill in the blanks with these words.

run   football   man   kick   off

1. Sam is a big _____.

2. Sam can _____.

3. He can _____.

4. He is not at work. He is _____.

5. Sam is good at _____.

Fill in the blanks with the letters *all*.
Read the words aloud.

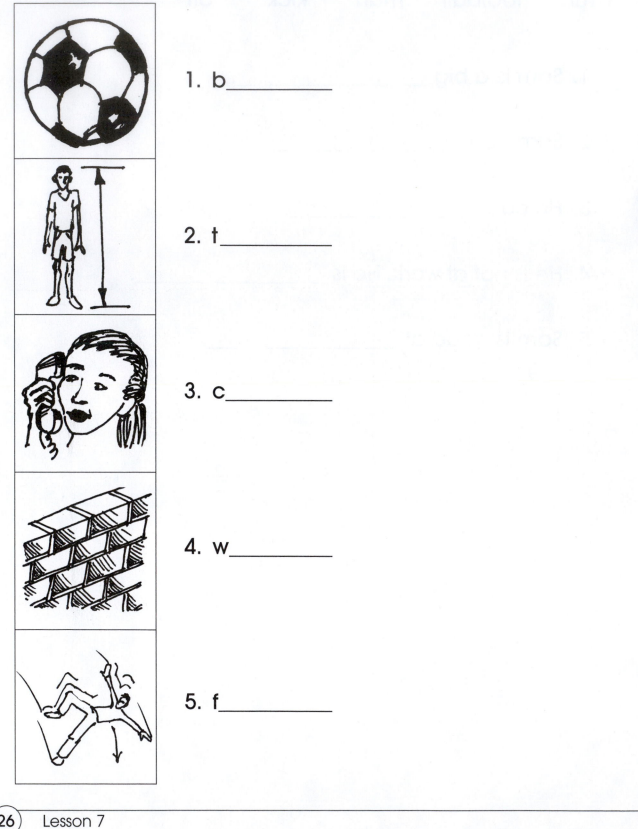

1. b_____

2. t_____

3. c_____

4. w_____

5. f_____

Listen. Fill in the blanks with these words.

back   lock   duck   lick   sock

kick   sick   clock   tack

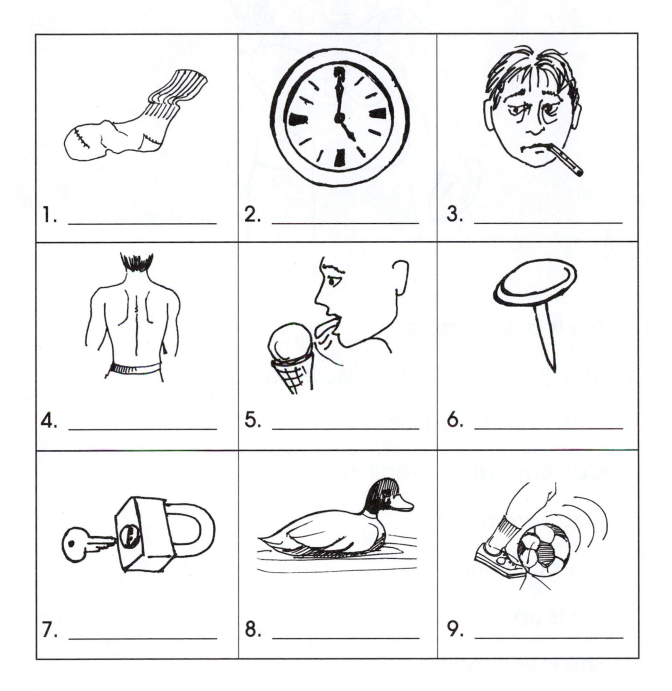

1. _____

2. _____

3. _____

4. _____

5. _____

6. _____

7. _____

8. _____

9. _____

Lesson

8 The Ball Is In!

🎧 1. Pat is at the game.

2. Run Sam, run! Pass the ball! Go Sam!

3. Sam has the last kick.

4. Can Sam get the ball in?

5. Can Sam miss?

6. The ball is in!

7. Pat is up.

8. She is very happy.

9. Sam and Pat hug and kiss.

**Read. Circle the correct word in the box.
Fill in the blanks.**

1. Kick the _____.

bal
ball

2. Sam and Pat _____.

kis
kiss

3. Sam has a _____.

bos
boss

4. The man is _____.

tal
tall

5. I am _____.

wel
well

6. Go up the _____.

hil
hill

7. It is a gas _____.

bil
bill

8. She can _____.

pas
pass

Fill in the blanks with these words.

in   kick   kiss   happy   miss

1. Sam has the last _____.

2. Sam can get the ball _____.

3. Can Sam _____?

4. Pat is very _____.

5. Sam and Pat hug and _____.

Listen and fill in the blanks with *ss*, *ff*, or *ll*.

1. bo __ __

2. o __ __

3. te __ __

4. ki __ __

5. be __ __

6. cu __ __

 **Listen and write.**

1. _____

2. _____

3. _____

4. _____

5. _____

6. _____

Lesson

9 Sam Can't Get Up

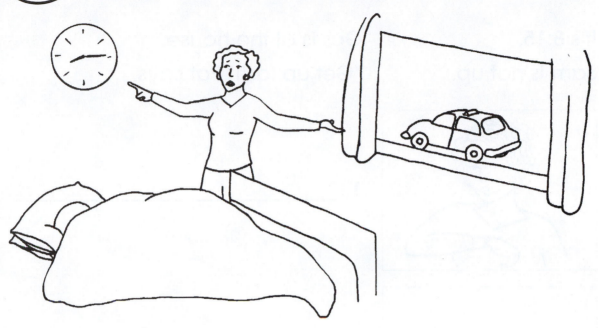

1. Gus can get Sam.

2. Sam can go with Gus in the taxi.

3. But it's 8:15 A.M.

4. Sam is not up.

5. Gus is at the house.

6. But Sam is not up.

7. "Come on, Sam," Pat says.

8. "Gus is here. Get up!"

9. "Get up fast!"

10. "It's 8:15."

Match the sentences with the pictures.
Write the sentences in the blanks.

It's 8:15.   Gus is at the house.
Sam is not up.   "Get up fast!" Pat says.

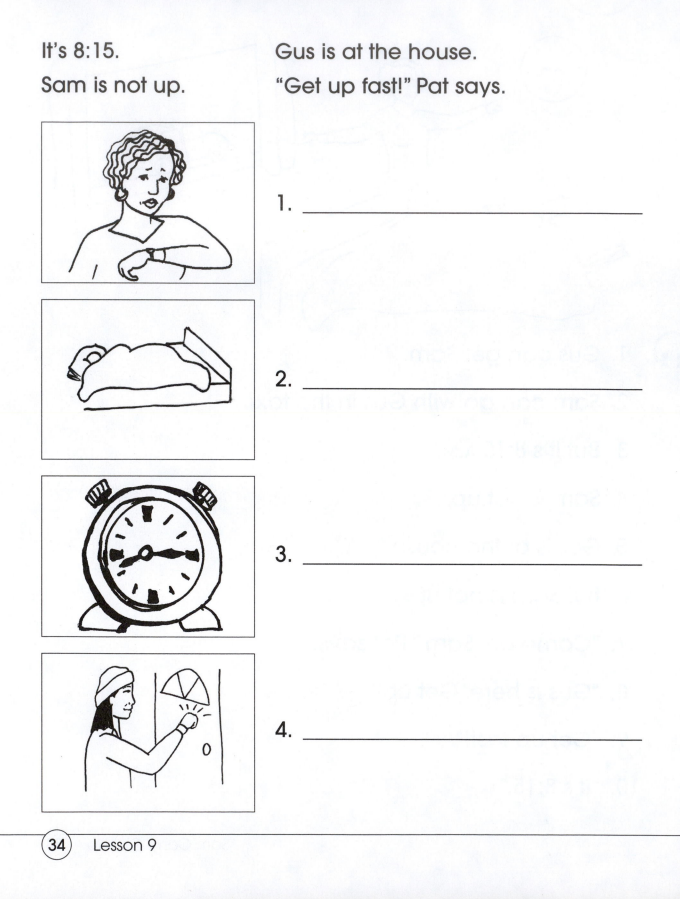

1. _____

2. _____

3. _____

4. _____

Listen and write the missing letters.

1. ____am

2. ____an

3. ____at

4. ____axi

5. ____at

6. ____us

7. ____ome

8. ____uck

9. ____ot

10. ____ut

11. ____an

12. ____un

13. ____ork

14. ____et

🎧 1. Sam is up fast.

2. He has to wash.

3. He has to put on his pants and shirt.

4. He has to put on his socks and shoes.

5. He has to put on his jacket and hat.

6. It is 8:30 A.M.

7. Gus is in the taxi.

8. Sam is in the taxi.

9. Gus and Sam go fast.

10. Is Sam late to work today?

Match the sentences with the pictures.
Write the sentences in the blanks.

Sam has to wash.

He has to put on his shoes.

Gus and Sam go fast.

He has to put on his shirt.

He has to put on his pants.

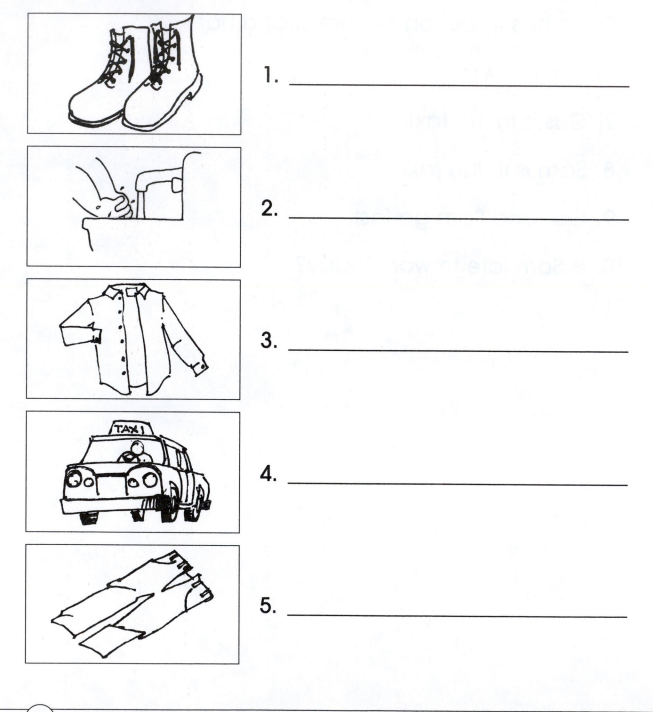

1. _____

2. _____

3. _____

4. _____

5. _____

Fill in the blanks with the letters *sh*.
Read the words aloud.

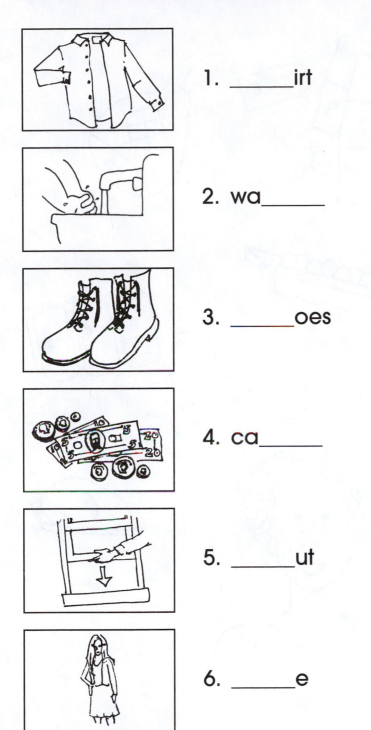

1. _____irt

2. wa_____

3. _____oes

4. ca_____

5. _____ut

6. _____e

Lesson

(11) Pat Shops on Saturday

1. Pat shops on Saturday.

2. Today she has to get eggs, milk, and chicken.

3. She has to get a ham for Sunday lunch.

4. Chips are on sale. Six bags for $1.00.

5. Pop is on sale. A six-pack for $2.00.

6. Pat gets six bags of chips.

7. She gets a six-pack of pop.

8. But the chips are not good for Sam.

9. The pop is not good for Sam.

10. Sam is too fat.

11. Pat puts the chips and the pop back.

Write Yes or No.

  1. Pat shops on Sunday.   _____

  2. Pat gets eggs and chicken.   _____

  3. Milk is on sale.   _____

  4. Chips are on sale.   _____

  5. A six-pack of pop is $2.00.   _____

  6. Chips are good for Sam.   _____

  7. Pat puts the chips back.   _____

Fill in the blanks with these words.

bags   sale   shops   back   fat

  1. Sam is too _____.

  2. Chips are on _____.

  3. Pat _____ on Saturday.

  4. Pat gets six _____ of chips.

  5. Pat puts the chips _____.

Match the words with the pictures.

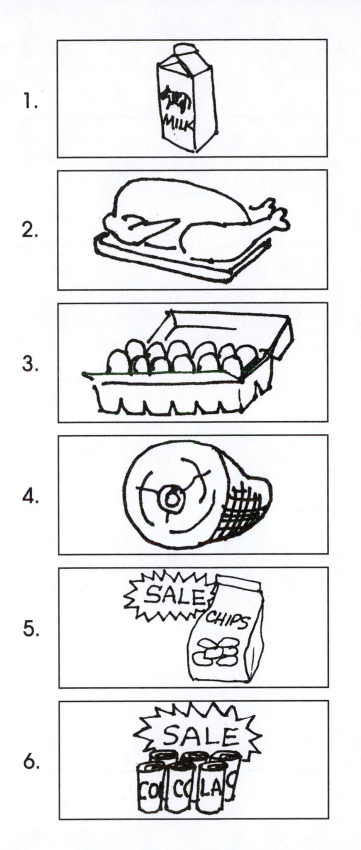

1. chips

2. eggs

3. pop

4. milk

5. ham

6. chicken

Write the words next to the pictures.

1. _____

2. _____

3. _____

4. _____

5. _____

6. _____

Read the words.   **Write the words again with _s_.**

1. egg   _____

2. can   _____

3. cup   _____

4. bag   _____

5. ham   _____

6. yam   _____

Lesson

12 Pat's Job

1. Pat works in a school.

2. It is a big school.

3. Her job is to fix lunch.

4. She can fix lunch for the kids.

5. Today she will fix fish sticks.

6. The kids come in at 11:30 A.M.

7. Fish sticks are good for the kids.

8. But the kids say, "Ick! Fish sticks!"

9. "Fish sticks stink!"

Write *Yes* or *No*.   **Yes or No**

1. Pat works in a taxi.   _____

2. Pat is a cook.   _____

3. She can fix fish sticks.   _____

4. The kids come in at 1:00 P.M.   _____

5. The kids say, "Yum! Fish sticks
   are good."   _____

Fill in the blanks with these words.

kick   pick   sticks   lick   sick

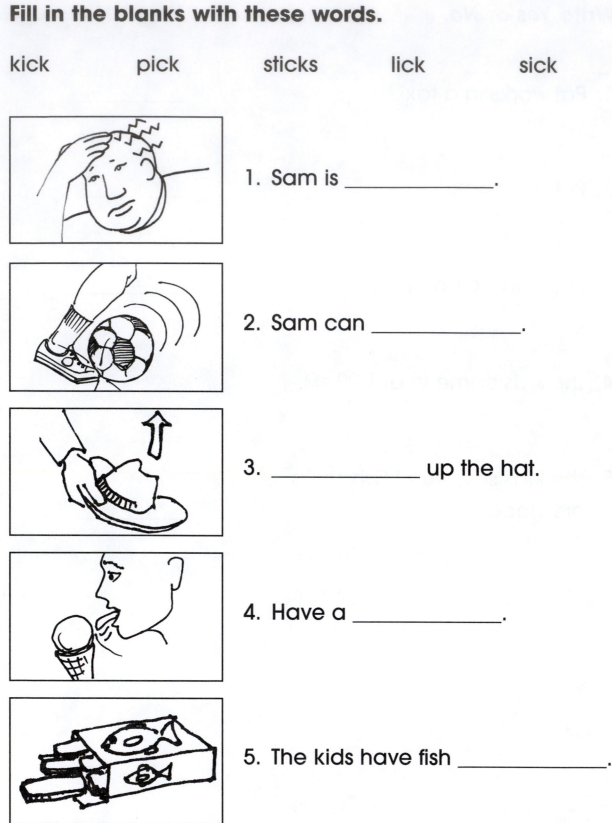

1. Sam is _____.

2. Sam can _____.

3. _____ up the hat.

4. Have a _____.

5. The kids have fish _____.

Fill in the blanks with these words.

tack   back   sack   black

1. The food is in the _____.

2. He sat on a _____.

3. This is a _____ cat.

4. This is her _____.

13 Go Home, Sam

🎧 1. It's Friday.

2. Gus has Sam in his taxi.

3. Gus and Sam go fast.

4. But they are late.

5. It's no good. Sam is late to work.

6. The boss says, "You can't come to work late."

7. "Go home, Sam."

8. It's Friday at 1:30 P.M.

9. Pat is at home.

10. Sam is in the kitchen.

11. He is sad.

12. "What is the matter?" Pat asks.

13. "I am fired," says Sam.

14. "The boss says I can't come back."

15. Sam says, "I'm sick."

16. Pat says, "You are not sick. You are mad."

17. Pat says, "I'm mad and sad too."

Circle the correct answers.

1. Pat works
in a bank.
in a school.
in a hotel.

2. Pat can fix
breakfast
dinner
lunch
for the kids.

3. Pat is at home at
1:30.
3:00.
4:30.

4. Sam is
happy.
fat.
sad and mad.

5. Sam is
at work.
in the kitchen.
at school.

6. It is
Friday.
Monday.
Sunday.

7. Pat is
sick.
happy.
sad.

Circle the words you hear.

1. sick   sit   sip   Sid

2. back   bat   bad   bag

3. bug   bus   but   bun

4. fish   fit   fix   fig

5. cash   cat   can   cap

6. run   rub   rush   rug

7. hit   him   his   hip

8. mash   mad   Mack   man

9. sun   sub   sum   suck

10. pin   pit   pick   pill

Lesson

14 It Is Very Expensive

🎧 1. Pat and Sam need help.

2. Pat can work.

3. But Sam has no job.

4. Pat and Sam need cash.

5. The rent is expensive.

6. The gas and the telephone are expensive.

7. They have a big bill for heat in December too.

8. Sam says, "This is too much!"

9. "I need a rest."

10. "I have to go to bed."

11. Pat says, "You are not sick. You are sad."

12. "Get up."

13. Sam says, "OK, OK. Get off my back!"

Read the story. Circle the answers.

1. Who needs help?

   Pat   Pat and Sam   Sam

2. Who needs cash?

   Pat   Pat and Sam   Sam

3. Who is sad?

   Pat   Sam   Gus

4. Who needs a rest?

   Pat   Sam   Pat and Sam

5. Who has big bills?

   Pat   Sam   Pat and Sam

Read the words. Underline the /e/ sounds.

1. help
2. expensive
3. rest
4. November
5. bed

6. rent
7. get
8. telephone
9. egg
10. December

Find 5 words in the story with /a/. Write the words.

1. _____

2. _____

3. _____

4. _____

5. _____

15 Gus and Sam Relax

🎧 1. Sam and Gus relax.

2. They sit on a rock and fish.

3. They fish all day.

4. Sam has good luck.

5. He gets ten big fish.

6. Gus has bad luck.

7. He gets one small fish.

8. Gus is sad.

9. "That's OK," says Sam.

10. "You can have my fish."

11. "We can cook fish at home."

12. "We can have fish and chips."

Write *Yes* or *No*.   ***Yes* or *No***

1. Gus and Sam relax.   _____

2. They sit on a log.   _____

3. Sam has bad luck.   _____

4. Gus is happy.   _____

5. Sam gets ten big fish.   _____

6. Gus and Sam work today.   _____

7. Sam is mad.   _____

Fill in the blanks with these words.

small   relax   fish   luck   home

1. He gets ten big _____.

2. Gus has bad _____.

3. He gets one _____ fish.

4. We can cook fish at _____.

5. Gus and Sam _____.

Lesson

16 Fish Smell

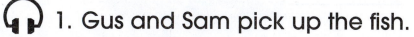 1. Gus and Sam pick up the fish.

2. They get in the van.

3. The van is hot.

4. The fish smell bad.

5. Sam and Gus have fish on their pants.

6. They have fish on their shoes.

7. They smell bad.

8. Gus and Sam get home.

9. Pat is in the kitchen.

10. She says, "You have fish on your pants."

11. "I can smell fish."

12. "Go wash. Take a bath."

Circle *Yes* or *No*.   ***Yes* or *No***

1. The van is cold.   Yes   No

2. The fish smell good.   Yes   No

3. They have fish on their shoes.   Yes   No

4. Pat is not at home.   Yes   No

5. Pat says, "You can cook the fish."   Yes   No

6. Sam has a bath.   Yes   No

Fill in the blanks with these words.

bad   pants   home   bath   hot

1. Sam and Gus have fish on their _____.

2. Gus and Sam get _____.

3. Take a _____.

4. The fish smell _____.

5. The van is _____.

Circle the words you hear.

1. shin   chin   thin

2. chip   ship   thick

3. dish   rich   bath

4. path   wish   rich

5. with   mash   chin

6. shut   thick   cash

7. shot   with   chip

**Listen to the words. Choose the correct letters.
Write the words.**

ck   sh   ch   th

1. pi ____   _____

2. lu ____   _____

3. fi ____   _____

4. ____ oes   _____

5. wa ____   _____

6. ba ____   _____

7. ____ ips   _____

8. ro ____   _____

Lesson

17 Buddy

1. Pat and Sam have a son.

2. His name is Buddy.

3. Buddy is 15.

4. Buddy is a good son.

5. Buddy has a trumpet.

6. He can play the trumpet very well.

7. He has a trumpet lesson every Wednesday.

8. He plays every night in bed.

9. The problem is Sam and Pat.

10. Sam and Pat can't rest.

11. Sam and Pat can't go to bed.

Fill in the blanks with these words.

rest   trumpet   Wednesday

Buddy   son   Sam

1. Pat and _____ have a son.

2. Buddy is the _____ .

3. Buddy can play the _____ very well.

4. Buddy has a trumpet lesson on _____ .

5. Every night _____ plays the trumpet.

6. Sam and Pat can't _____ .

Fill in the blanks with the correct words.

rest   best

1. Sam and Pat can't _____.

2. This is Buddy's _____ friend.

---

neck   check

3. This is her _____.

4. This _____ is for rent.

---

pen   ten

5. This is a _____.

6. This is _____.

---

pet   get

7. They _____ on the bus.

8. A cat is a good _____.

Listen. Fill in the missing letters.

Copy the words. Read.

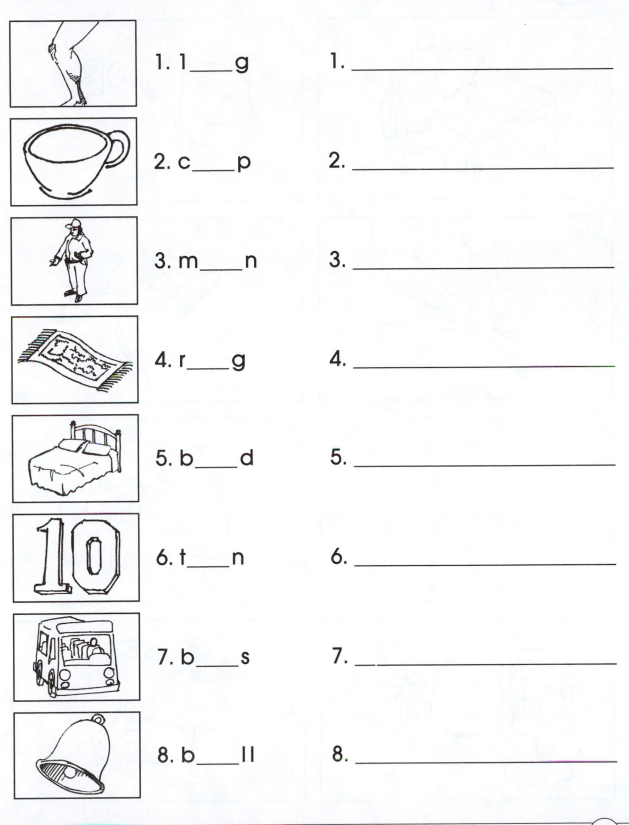

1. l___g

2. c___p

3. m___n

4. r___g

5. b___d

6. t___n

7. b___s

8. b___ll

1. _____

2. _____

3. _____

4. _____

5. _____

6. _____

7. _____

8. _____

 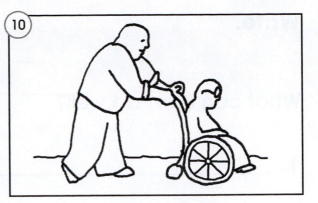

1. Sam has to get a job.

2. What is a good job for Sam?

3. What can Sam do well?

4. Sam can cook.

5. He is good with his hands.

6. He can fix things.

7. He is a big man, and he has a good back.

8. He can lift big things.

9. Sam can work well with people.

10. He can work with cash and checks.

11. He can clean.

12. He can work with sick people.

Write.

What can Sam do well?

1. _____

   _____

2. _____

   _____

3. _____

   _____

4. _____

   _____

5. _____

   _____

Write.

What can you do well?

_____

_____

_____

_____

_____

_____

_____

_____

_____

_____

Fill in the blanks with the correct words.

van   pan

1. This is a _____.

2. This is a _____.

---

sit   hit

3. They _____ on the bed.

4. The van _____ the taxi.

---

mug   hug

5. Pat and Sam _____.

6. This is a _____.

hat   fat

7. This is a _____.

8. This cat is _____.

pin   chin

9. This is a _____.

10. This is his _____.

luck   duck

11. She has good _____.

12. This is a _____.

Lesson

19 Sam Gets a Job

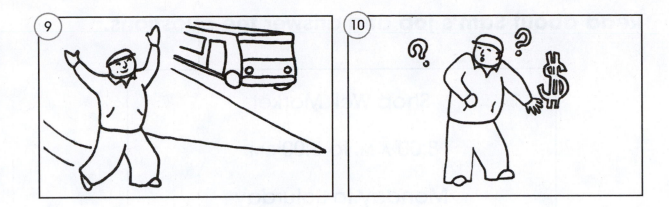

1. Sam is at the Shop Well Market.

2. Sam thinks, "Maybe they have a job for me."

3. He asks for a job.

4. He talks to the boss.

5. Sam says, "I can mop."

6. "I can bag."

7. "I can help with stock."

8. The boss has a job for Sam.

9. He says, "You can start on Monday."

10. "You can work from 8:00 A.M. to 3:00 P.M."

11. Sam is very happy.

12. He runs to get the bus.

13. But he stops.

14. He forgot to ask.

15. What is the pay?

Read about Sam's job and answer the questions.

```
Shop Well Market

8:00 A.M. to 3:00 P.M.

Monday to Saturday

Mop the floor, help with stock, bag

$6.50/hour
```

1. What market? _____

2. What days? _____

3. What time? _____

4. What work? _____

_____

5. What pay? _____

Write the sentences next to the correct pictures.

Sam can mop.   He can help with stock.

He can bag.   Sam runs to get the bus.

Then he stops.

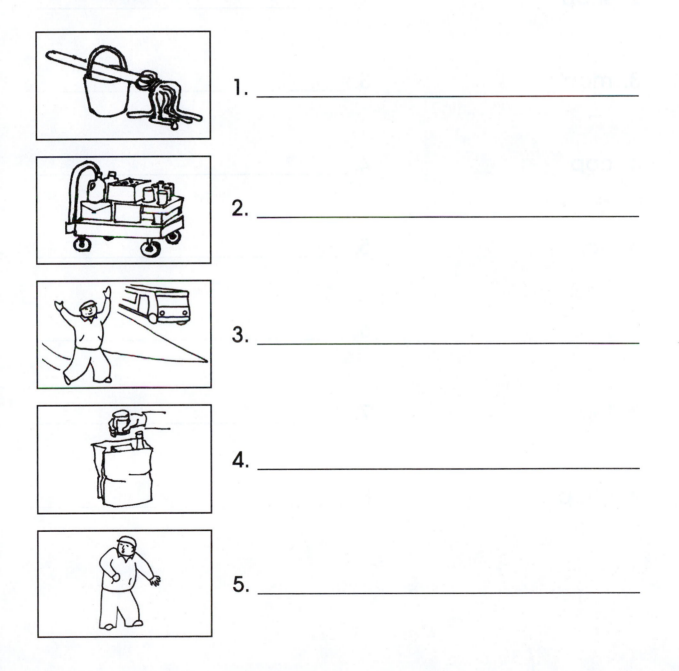

1. _____

2. _____

3. _____

4. _____

5. _____

Read the words.   **Listen and write the words again.**

1. stop   1. _____

2. shop   2. _____

3. mop   3. _____

4. cop   4. _____

5. hop   5. _____

6. pop   6. _____

7. top   7. _____

8. chop   8. _____

Read the words.   **Listen and write the words again.**

1. hot

2. pot

3. lot

4. not

5. shot

6. dot

1. _____

2. _____

3. _____

4. _____

5. _____

6. _____

Read these words.

1. stop   5. fast

2. stock   6. rest

3. stay   7. dust

4. stick   8. fast

Listen and circle the words you hear.

1. sop   stop

2. sock   stock

3. say   stay

4. sick   stick

_____

5. fast   fat

6. best   bet

7. cast   cat

8. fast   fat

Lesson

20 Sam Tells Pat the Good News

Sam: Pat! I have a job at the Shop Well Market!

Pat: Good, Sam! Good, good, very, very good!
        What day can you start?

Sam: I can start on Monday.

Pat: What time?

Sam: I work from 8:00 A.M. to 3:00 P.M.

Pat: What is the job?

Sam: I mop. I bag. I help with stock.

Pat: What is the pay?

Sam: Oh, no! I forgot to ask!

Fill in the blanks with these words.

What   start   job   help   forgot

1. Sam has a _____.

2. Sam can _____ on Monday.

3. Sam can _____ with stock.

4. _____ is the pay?

5. Sam _____ to ask!

What is a good job for you?

A good job for me is _____.

Good pay is _____.

I can work _____.
                                    (days)

I can work _____.
                                    (time)

Copy your story.

_____

_____

_____

_____

_____

Circle the words you hear.

1. sit   pit   spit

2. sell   tell   spell

3. slip   sip   lip

4. pool   stool   spool

5. pill   sill   spill

6. smell   spell   sell

7. sick   stick   tick

8. slap   sap   lap

9. top   pop   stop

10. sock   stock   sick

11. spot   pot   sit

12. sin   pin   spin

Fill in the blanks with the correct words.

fast	last	dust	rest
stock	stop	stick	stay

1. This is a bus _____.

2. This is a _____.

3. Sam can run _____.

4. This man is _____.

5. Sam can help with _____ in the market.

6. Go to bed and _____.

7. You have to _____ home.

8. Clean up the _____.

Lesson

(21) Pat Is in New York

1. Pat is in New York.

2. She has a brother in New York.

3. His name is Tom.

4. Pat is in New York to see Tom.

5. Pat has to get a cab.

6. But the cabs do not stop.

7. "Maybe I can take a bus? What bus?"

8. Pat is lost.

9. She has to get a map.

10. Pat sees a small shop.

11. Maps are expensive!

12. They cost a lot. $8.00! That is too much.

13. Pat has to have cash for a cab.

14. Pat asks a cop for help.

15. "Get a cab," the cop says.

16. "But the cabs do not stop!"

17. The cop calls a cab for Pat.

18. Pat says, "Thanks a lot!"

19. She gets in the cab.

20. Pat says, "I love New York!"

Write *Yes* or *No*.   ***Yes* or *No***

1. Pat has a sister in New York.   _____

2. She has to get a van.   _____

3. Pat is lost.   _____

4. Pat is in Boston.   _____

5. She has to get a map.   _____

6. Pat asks a cook for help.   _____

Fill in the blanks with these words.

cab   stop   has   Tom   in   lost

1. Pat _____ a brother.

2. His name is _____.

3. Pat is _____ New York.

4. Pat is _____.

5. The cabs do not _____.

6. A cop gets a _____ for Pat.

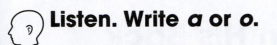

Listen. Write _a_ or _o_.

1. c__b

2. p__t

3. r__n

4. P__t

5. j__ck

6. l__ck

7. m__p

(22) Sam Has a Pain in His Back

1. It is Thursday. Sam is not at work.

2. Sam is off on Thursday.

3. It is good that Sam does not have work today.

4. Sam has a bad pain in his back.

5. He has a pain in his hip.

6. He has a pain in his neck.

7. He has a pain in his leg too.

8. Sam is in bed.

9. He has a lot of things to do.

10. But he can't get up.

11. Sam has to take pills for the pain.

12. The pills do not help.

13. The pills do not fix his back.

14. Pat says, "Call the doctor."

15. "Doctor King can help you."

16. "You can go to Doctor King."

17. "Doctor King can help you get well."

18. "Call the doctor today!"

19. Sam says, "OK, OK. Don't get mad."

20. "I will call Doctor King today."

Write *Yes* or *No*.   **Yes or No**

1. Sam has to work on Thursday.   _____

2. Sam has a pain in his back.   _____

3. Sam has a pain in his chest.   _____

4. Sam is in bed.   _____

5. He has nothing to do.   _____

6. He can't get up.   _____

7. The pills do not help.   _____

8. Sam will call Doctor King.   _____

Read the sentences on pages 97-98.
Write the correct sentences next to these pictures.

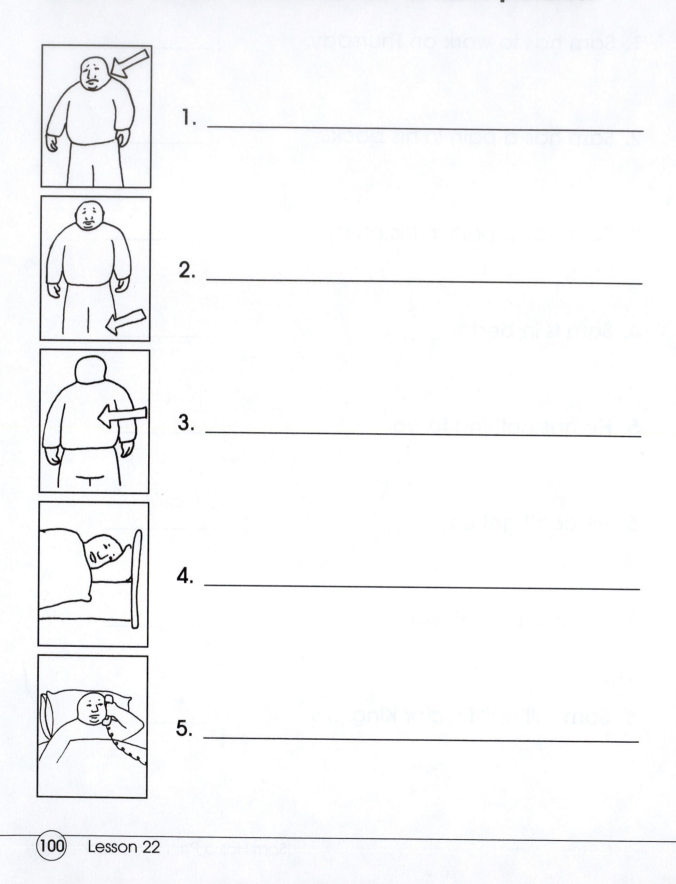

1. _____

2. _____

3. _____

4. _____

5. _____

Fill in *ing*.
Read the words.

Write the words.

1. k_____   _____

2. s_____   _____

3. w_____   _____

4. th_____   _____

5. r_____   _____

Read the words. Write the words with *s.*

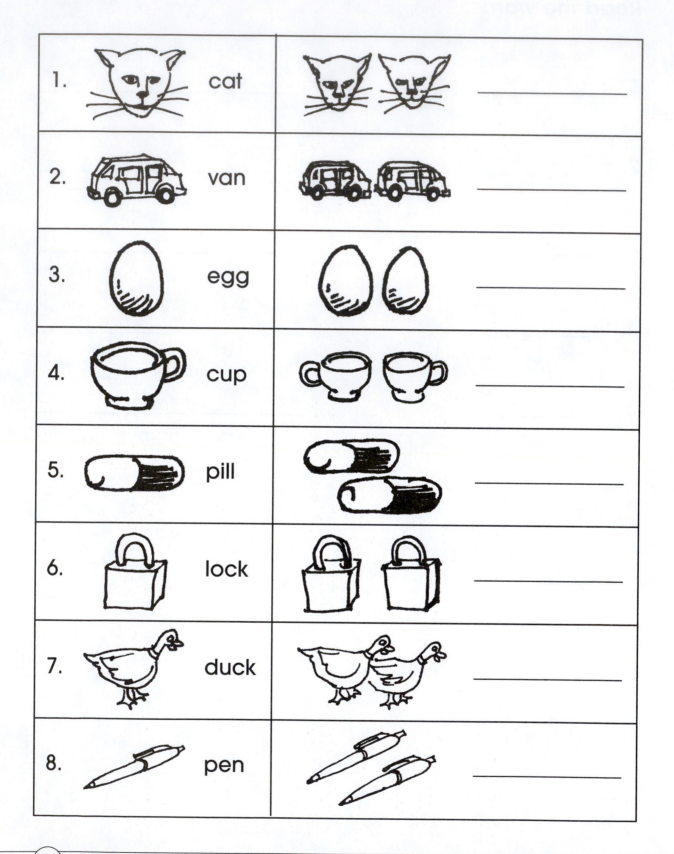

1.		cat		_____
2.		van		_____
3.		egg		_____
4.		cup		_____
5.		pill		_____
6.		lock		_____
7.		duck		_____
8.		pen		_____

Phonetic Word Grids

Phonetic Word Grid 1

Name: _____

man   hat   sad   dad   van

ham   mad   fat   pan   rat

1. _____

2. _____

3. _____

4. _____

5. _____

6. _____

7. _____

8. _____

9. _____

10. _____

Phonetic Word Grid 2

Name: _____

run   cut   gum   hug   cup   rug
sun   mug   bus   tub   bug   pup

1. _____

2. _____

3. _____

4. _____

5. _____

6. _____

7. _____

8. _____

9. _____

10. _____

11. _____

12. _____

Phonetic Word Grid 3

Name: _____

back   hug   bag   duck   cat   jump
lamp   can   plug   run   bus   man

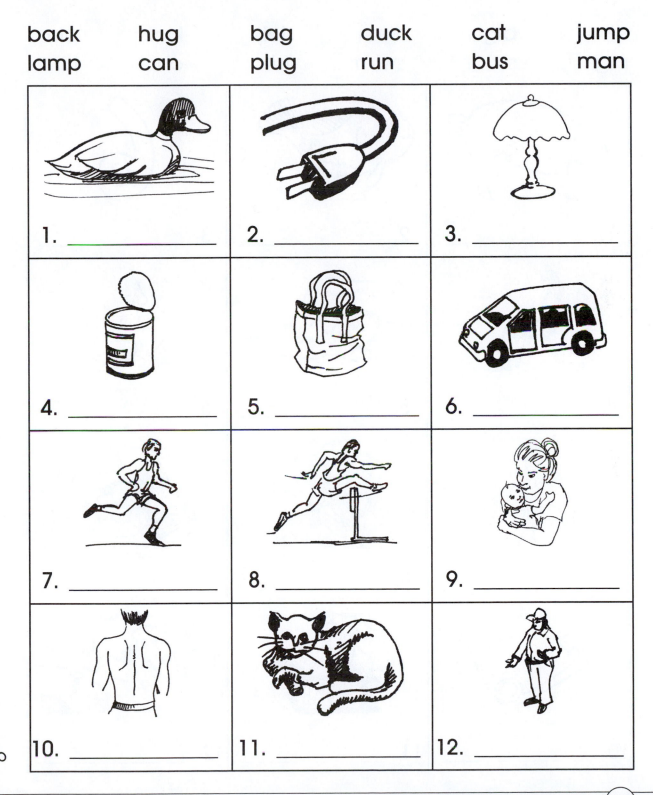

1. _____

2. _____

3. _____

4. _____

5. _____

6. _____

7. _____

8. _____

9. _____

10. _____

11. _____

12. _____

Phonetic Word Grid 4

Name: _____

sit	big	thin	sick	kick	pin
pig	six	swim	fish	chin	hit

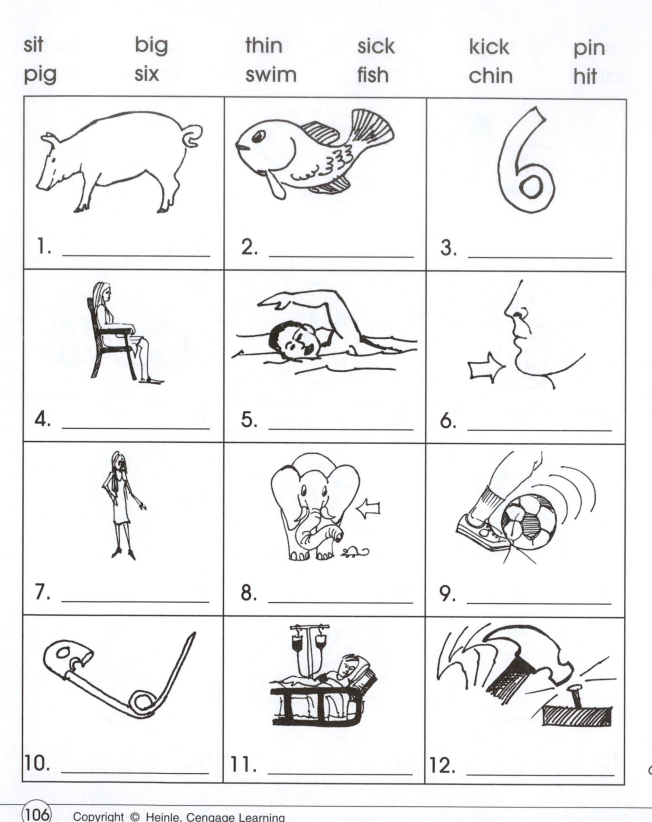

1. _____

2. _____

3. _____

4. _____

5. _____

6. _____

7. _____

8. _____

9. _____

10. _____

11. _____

12. _____

Phonetic Word Grid 5

Name: _____

bed   leg   pen   ten   belt
check   dress   egg   bell   desk

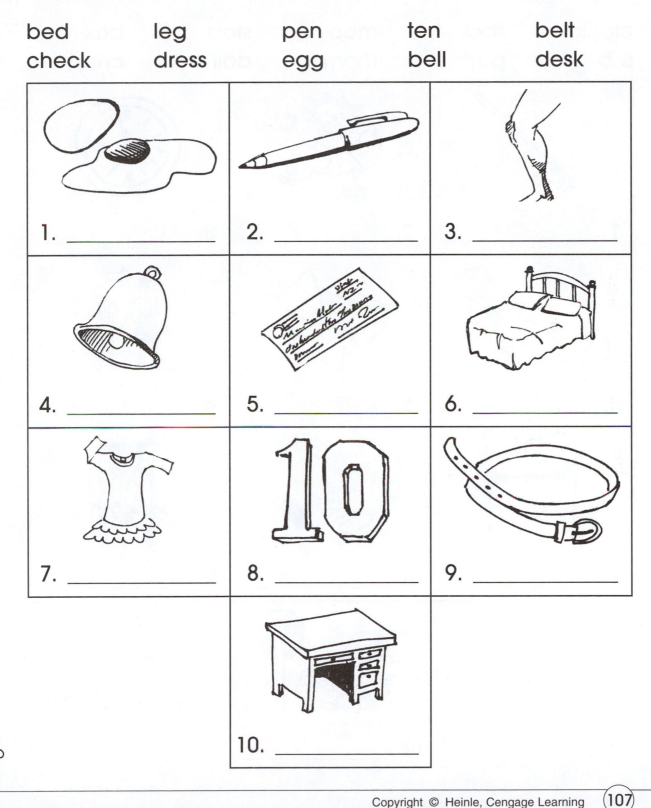

1. _____   2. _____   3. _____

4. _____   5. _____   6. _____

7. _____   8. _____   9. _____

10. _____

Phonetic Word Grid 6

Name: _____

clock	sock	mop
rob	pot	mom

stop	box	
doll	chop	

1. _____

2. _____

3. _____

4. _____

5. _____

6. _____

7. _____

8. _____

9. _____

10. _____

Phonetic Word Grid 7

Name: _____

step   spit   spill   smell   stop
spin   slip   slam   slim

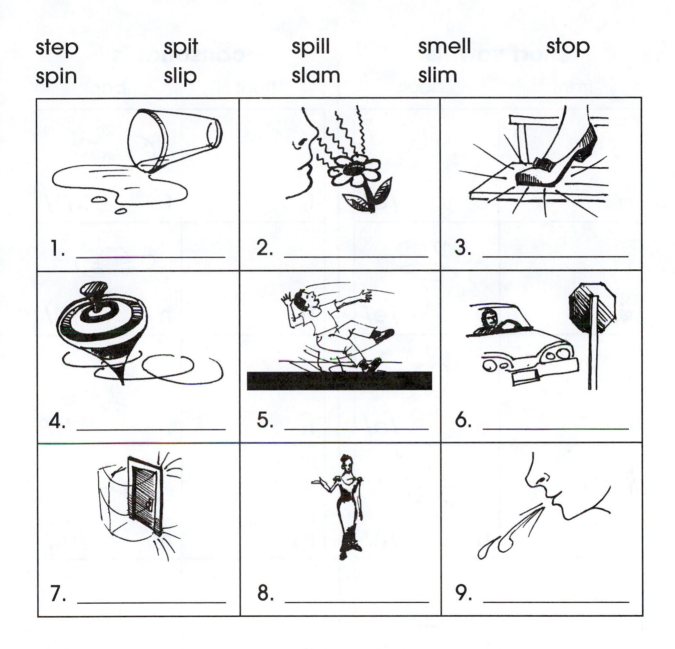

1. _____

2. _____

3. _____

4. _____

5. _____

6. _____

7. _____

8. _____

9. _____

Key Word Cards for Phonics

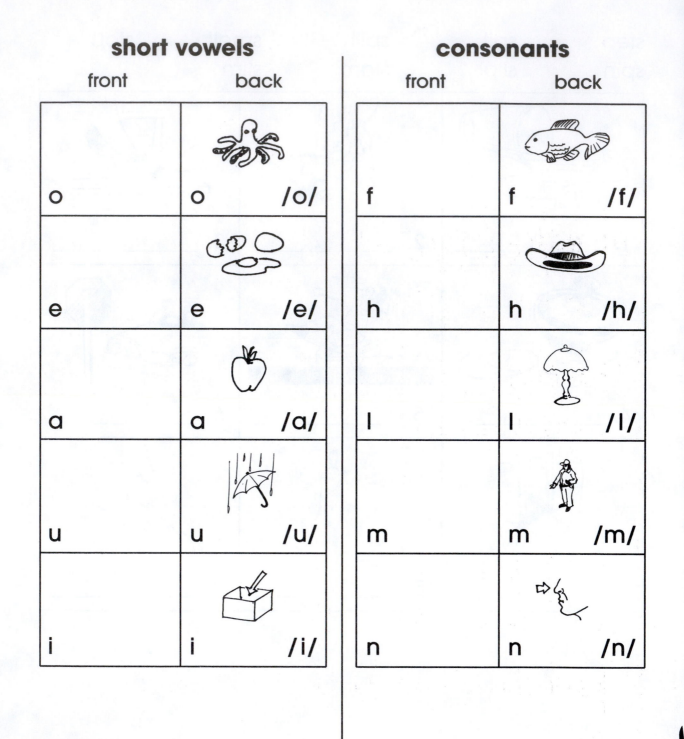

short vowels

front	back
o	o /o/
e	e /e/
a	a /a/
u	u /u/
i	i /i/

consonants

front	back
f	f /f/
h	h /h/
l	l /l/
m	m /m/
n	n /n/

Key Word Cards for Phonics

consonants

front	back
r	r /r/
s	s /s/
v	v /v/
z	z /z/
b	b /b/

consonants

front	back
c	c /c/
d	d /d/
g	g /g/
j	j /j/
k	k /k/

Key Word Cards for Phonics

consonants		consonant digraphs	
front	**back**	**front**	**back**
p	p /p/	th	th /th/
qu	qu /qu/	sh	sh /sh/
t	t /t/	ch	ch /ch/
w	w /w/		
y	y /y/		
x	x /x/		

Suggested Listening Scripts

Listening activities ar indicated by this icon: ☺. The teacher can either use the **Suggested Listening Scripts** that are found here, or choose appropriate words that go with the lesson for dictation. These words should reinforce the phonetic element of the lesson. In addition, the **Phonetic Word Grids** can be assigned for supplemental practice as each new sound is introduced. They are listed in the **Lesson Chart** at the beginning of the book.

Page 3 Listen and write the missing letters.

1. Sam	5. Sam
2. Pat	6. Pat
3. mat	7. fan
4. pan	8. man

Page 3 Listen and write.

1. fat	4. pan
2. man	5. mat
3. Pat	

Page 7 Listen and write the missing letters.

1. can	6. can't
2. pan	7. hat
3. man	8. van
4. class	9. good
5. gas	10. cook

Page 10 Circle the words you hear.

1. hat	6. pad
2. rag	7. an
3. cap	8. sad
4. ham	9. bat
5. mat	10. tap

Page 11 Write the words you hear.

1. sad	4. man
2. bag	5. tap
3. cat	6. am

Page 31 Listen and fill in the blanks with *ss, ff,* or *ll.*

1. boss	4. kiss
2. off	5. bell
3. tell	6. cuff

Page 32 Listen and write.

1. tell	4. off
2. boss	5. bell
3. cuff	6. kiss

Page 35 Listen and write the missing letters.

1. Sam	8. luck
2. tan	9. hot
3. fat	10. nut
4. taxi	11. pan
5. mat	12. run
6. bus	13. work
7. come	14. get

Page 53 Circle the words you hear.

1. sick
2. bat
3. bun
4. fish
5. cap
6. rub
7. hip
8. Mack
9. sum
10. pill

Page 66 Circle the words you hear.

1. thin
2. chip
3. dish
4. path
5. mash
6. thick
7. with

Page 67 Listen to the words. Choose the correct letters. Write the words.

1. pick
2. luck
3. fish
4. shoes
5. wash
6. bath
7. chips
8. rock

Page 82 Read the words. Listen and write the words again.

Have the students cover the left hand column while you dictate the words.

Page 83 Read the words. Listen and write the words again.

Have the students cover the left hand column while you dictate the words.

Page 84 Listen and circle the words you hear.

1. stop
2. sock
3. say
4. stick
5. fat
6. best
7. cast
8. fast

Page 88 Circle the words you hear.

1. pit
2. sell
3. slip
4. pool
5. spill
6. smell
7. sick
8. slap
9. stop
10. stock
11. spot
12. sin

Page 95 Listen. Write *a* or *o*.

1. cab
2. pot
3. ran
4. Pat
5. jack
6. lock
7. mop